Cleveland Transit Through the Years

by

Blaine S. Hays
&
James A. Toman

© CLEVELAND LANDMARKS PRESS, INC., 1999

PUBLISHING INFORMATION

PUBLISHED BY:
CLEVELAND LANDMARKS PRESS, INC.
13610 SHAKER BOULEVARD, SUITE 503
CLEVELAND, OHIO 44120-1592

© 1999, CLEVELAND LANDMARKS PRESS, INC.

ISBN: 0-936760-14-1

DESIGNED BY:
RUSTY SCHNEIDER
MOONLIGHT PUBLISHING
HINCKLEY, OHIO

PRINTED BY:
BOOKMASTERS, INC.
MANSFIELD, OHIO

Acknowledgments

Clevelanders interested in the history of their city's public transportation system are fortunate. During the course of this past century, many photographers devoted considerable time and energy to capture the transit developments that were taking place. Their work has encouraged us to carry on the tradition in more recent times and has also prompted us to make sure that their historic record might become more widely known and appreciated.

A small sampling of the work of some of those photographers appears here. We are grateful to all of them and salute the contribution which they have made to recording a piece of Cleveland history. In particular, we salute Doc Rollins, Ross Barnard, Harry Christiansen, Jim Spangler, Roy Bruce, Tony Krisak, Bill Vigrass, Herb Harwood, Bob Runyon, and Bruce Young.

We also thank the principals in Cleveland Landmarks Press for their support of this project: Dan and Cathy Cook, and Greg Deegan. Our thanks also goes out to Rusty Schneider for layout and design, to Steve Heister and Bettye Morgan for their help, and to Joan Hays for her patience.

Front Cover Photo: A CTS streetcar during the last days of operation of the Madison Avenue car line is headed for Spring Garden Avenue in December 1953, while overhead work is underway on the new rapid transit line that will keep the traction tradition alive in Cleveland. *(Harry Christiansen photo, Gerald Brookins Museum of Electric Railways collection)*

Title Page Photo: This experimental car was on display at the 1934 Cleveland transit industry convention. *(Blaine Hays collection)*

Rear Cover Photo: The Kingsbury Shop yard of the Regional Transit Authority's Shaker Rapid lines came alive with colorful PCC cars during the period before the lines were totally rebuilt. August 1978. *(Blaine Hays photo)*

CTS articulated streetcar 5024 is on the private right-of-way on the Hayden-East 140th Street branch of the Euclid Avenue car line. The scene dates from summer 1948. *(Jim Spangler photo)*

Introduction

As the 20th century comes to an end, the Greater Cleveland metropolitan area is home to almost as many automobiles as it is to people. The area is crisscrossed by a network of super-highways, enabling people to easily and quickly move about the area without regard to bus routes or schedules. The convenience of using one's car to get to work, to go shopping, or to visit friends has relegated public transportation to a second class status. Today less than 15% of area commuters are regular users of the public transit system.

That was not always the case, however. During the first half of the century, public transit was king. The amount of print space the daily newspapers devoted to transit topics in those days amply testifies to just how important the daily streetcar or bus ride was in the lives of their readers. The World War II years were the last great hurrah for public transit. In Cleveland during those years, the several different transit systems in the county carried nearly a half-billion passengers a year. At the close of the century, that number has dwindled to about 60 million.

This photo essay looks at some of Cleveland's transit highlights during the 20th century. Cleveland played a leading role in transit developments during the first part of the century, and its system was widely admired. At the start of the century, there was a vigorous contest over who would control the local transit franchise. By 1910 that issue had been decided by court action, and the Cleveland Railway Company (CRC), a private concern, took over the city's streetcar network. The era of private control ended in 1942 when the Cleveland Railway Company gave way to the municipally controlled Cleveland Transit System (CTS). In 1975 CTS and the other independent transit operators of Cuyahoga County were absorbed in the Greater Cleveland Regional Transit Authority, which remains the county's public transit operator.

Not only did ownership of public transit change over the course of the century, but so too did the system's fleet of vehicles. It evolved from a fleet of all electric-powered streetcars, to a mixed one, supplemented by gasoline-powered buses and electric trackless trolleys, to one today that is primarily operated by diesel- and natural gas-fueled buses. During the century, riders saw the interurban network come and go, and a rail rapid transit system come and stay.

We hope this short essay captures the flavor of some of the city's transit developments, and that the photos illuminate not only the kinds of vehicles that people depended on, but also some of the cityscape through which they navigated. Most of the vehicles depicted here are long gone, and much of the city's face has been greatly changed. If this narrative rekindles some fond memories of those vanished times, places, and events, then it will have fulfilled its mission. It is good to remember.

Streetcars and double-deck buses share the roadways around Public Square in 1926. The double deck buses were good crowd carriers, with 62 seats, but they were not popular with riders who had to climb to the second deck. *(Cleveland Railway photo, Blaine Hays collection)*

To accommodate the heavy increase in passengers during World War II, CTS utilized a small fleet of wooden bus trailers. Two of the units are laying over at the end of the Wade Park line. *(Cleveland Transit System photo, Blaine Hays collection)*

Only a few of Cleveland's streetcar lines had reserved rights-of-way. Here a Mayfield Road streetcar is inbound on the Euclid Heights Boulevard center reservation in 1948. *(Bill Vigrass photo)*

Seven streetcars, three buses, and one trackless trolley crowd this Public Square scene. It is September 1946, Cleveland's all time high-ridership year, when 493 million passengers kept the system humming. *(Cleveland Press photo, Blaine Hays collection)*

Streetcar Designs for a Century of Transit

Watching a streetcar rolling down a Cleveland street before 1912 was much like watching one roll down the street of any major city. A distinct style had not yet come to the city, which by 1923 would evolve with the most recognizable transit fleet in the midwest.

Cleveland's leadership in transit vehicle development resulted from the coming together of three men whose strength of will and practical ideas for economical operation of transit services created procedures and designs later copied throughout the industry.

Preceding these men, however, were two others who laid some groundwork. One was J. A. Mehling, the first to design a streetcar with a door in the center of the body. His car, number 288, was built in the shops of the East Cleveland Railway Company in 1892, and by 1896 the concept had advanced to the point where Mehling could sell his rights of manufacture to the local street-car-building firm, which would later feature the center-door car as the focus of its entire line of city-type passenger cars.

The other early contributor was an out-of-towner named Thomas E. Mitten, who struggled to modernize the fleets of several large eastern cities—most notably Philadelphia. He introduced a front-entrance city car in 1911. Its advent ended years of accidents involving persons boarding at the rear, when the motorman, without a clear view, all too often would pull away from the stop prematurely.

Taking their cues from these two pioneers, three Clevelanders would remake and considerably improve the course for transit expansion. They were Gustave Kuhlman, John Stanley, and Peter Witt.

Gustave Kuhlman began his career in his family's furniture manufacturing business on St. Clair Street. He later expanded into carriage and streetcar body construction, first in the Broadway and Aetna neighborhood, and then to new and spacious buildings in Collinwood. From that location the G. C. Kuhlman Company became a major streetcar producer, and its products were the choice of Cleveland Railway.

Peter Witt served in several Cleveland political capacities. As city clerk during the administration of Mayor Tom L. Johnson, he was exposed to details of street railway operations first hand. Johnson, a transit operator himself, had waged war with Cleveland Electric Railway over the fares they charged. Witt's attention to detail and knowledge of transit led to his being appointed street railway commissioner on January 1, 1912.

Using ideas he gained as commissioner, Witt designed the "Car Rider's Car," so called because of its features of faster loading and easier fare collection. He personally supervised construction of the first model in Cleveland Railway's Lakeview Shops in 1914. Later, when Witt sold rights for the construction of his cars to properties in other cities, they became known as "Peter Witt Cars."

John Stanley began his transit career working for the Cleveland Electric Railway Company, and after additional transit experience elsewhere, he returned to Cleveland in 1902 as general manager of Cleveland Electric Railway, a fortunate event for the future of transit in Cleveland. Stanley believed that if a company was going to run streetcars, they should be large streetcars, and if it was going to run trailer streetcars, they should be long trailers. In Cleveland, he was to preside over some of the longest motor-trailer combinations ever seen in the industry.

John Stanley's sound operation of public transit, combined with the superb operational ideas of Commissioner Witt and the quality car construction by G. C. Kuhlman led Cleveland to be an industry innovation leader. Even Thomas Mitten, when he later refined the style of his city streetcars, adopted the Peter Witt car plan.

Field observation using the new type car led Stanley and Witt to develop the skip-stop operation of streetcars, whereby every other trip would stop at alternating stops, thus reducing dwell time. Witt's perfection, in 1912, of the "pay-as-you-pass" rather than the "pay-as-you-enter" boarding practice allowed passengers to quickly board a car. Passengers could either pay the fare to the conductor at the center door and sit in the rear, or move to the front of the car and pay when disembarking. This system, joined by Stanley's longer cars, shortened running times to such an extent that transit operation was revolutionized and subsequently copied around the world.

In 1906, prior to Cleveland adopting distinctive transit vehicle styles, cars like this handsome deck roof convertible car traveled the streets. Thousands of front and rear entrance/exit city streetcars like this one were made for cities across the nation. *(Cleveland Railway photo, Blaine Hays collection)*

This is the center-entrance car which started it all: the original East Cleveland Railway number 288 and its new concept of unloading from the center. After refinements, originator J.A. Mehling sold the rights of manufacture to G.C. Kuhlman. *(Eugene Schmidt collection, Northern Ohio Railway Museum)*

Car number 33, the original Peter Witt car of 1914, is seen when new with its front entrance and center exit and Scullin louver roof. A later improvement was to widen the front doors for faster loading. *(Blaine Hays collection)*

Tom L. Johnson's long Cincinnati- built deck roof car at Payne Station in 1908, before rebuilding. *(Cleveland Railway photo, Blaine Hays collection)*

Shown at from Denison Station when first rebuilt in 1915, this is car 901 as a Peter Witt. *(Cleveland Railway photo, Blaine Hays collection)*

Operating Techniques for the Transit Age

In 1903 the Cleveland Electric Railway broke the 100,000,000-rider mark, leading General Manager John Stanley to ponder how better to serve the increasing passenger tally. His first move was to order two long trailer cars to test their practicality. They were the prelude to a decade in which both motor cars and trailer cars grew longer. That trend culminated in 1910 with the 900 series, the first streetcars ordered by Cleveland Electric Railway's successor, the Cleveland Railway Company. These cars were a whopping 52' 6" in length. In 1912 the company placed an order for 100 trailer cars (2000-2099) which were 49' 3" long.

In the meantime, an in-house talent was perfecting some ideas for another style of streetcar. Under the watchful eye of John Stanley, in 1911 Cleveland Railway master mechanic Terrance Scullin headed up the construction of a high-floor type car, number 824. His car featured rear door pay-as-you-enter (PAYE) fare collection. The front-exit rear-entrance car had a small clerestory mounted on a high arched roof which acted to protect roof vents from rain. The design produced improved airflow in the car, and it became known as the Scullin Louver Roof. The other feature of the car involved the wheels. The large 34" wheels were mounted on trucks with outside hung motors. This design enabled cars to take curves and pull trailers while producing very little screeching.

In 1913 Cleveland Railway placed an order with the Kuhlman Car Company for long 51' center-entrance motor cars (1100-1149) to be equipped with the Scullin roof. They were matched up with the long 1912-built trailers. Cleveland Railway found the cars quite satisfactory, and ultimately ordered a total of 201 car in the series, the largest fleet of streetcars ever ordered by the company.

Kuhlman got the chance to feature its center-entrance design not only in these cars but also in an experimental subway car it constructed in June 1913 for the Cleveland Underground Subway Company which was planning a subway under Euclid Avenue (the subway was never built, and the car remained a one-of-a-kind design).

In order to introduce its trailer-train concept, Cleveland Railway converted some older former motor cars to trailers and pulled them with similar-looking motor cars. Then the company took some of its newest non-center-entrance cars, 900-925, (which were 52' 8" long) and rebuilt them into the Peter Witt style with a center door. These cars had been purchased in the Municipal Traction days of Tom L. Johnson and were the newest cars owned by the merged company when it took over operations on March 1, 1910.

The trend all through the early years of the century was toward long, classically styled motor cars with matching trailers. By the mid-1920's the style became synonymous with Cleveland operation. The handsome and distinctive streetcars fit in well with the city's prevailing architecture.

Railroad-roof trailer 2043 from the first large group of "John Stanley" trailers at Windermere Station shortly after delivery. Note the instruction to "pay as you leave" in both the front and center windows. Car is being pulled by one of the old-style 100's. *(Blaine Hays collection)*

Cleveland Railway car 824 had been in an accident in 1911 and was scrapped and at the same time Terrence Scullin was building his new louver roof car. It received number 824 as a fill-in number but later became a prototype car for the highfloor fleet and was eventually renumbered 1052, the very last car in the "ten-hundred" fleet (1000-1052). This builder's photo was probably taken at Windermere Station just prior to the first run. *(Blaine Hays collection)*

The great trailer-train era has begun in Cleveland. It is the winter of 1914 and 1107 is just days from Kuhlman with its Eclipse fender and six-month-old railroad-roof trailer 2179 in tow. The scene is at Superior Station, a picture perfect image of Cleveland Railway operations. *(Blaine Hays collection)*

This is the prototype subway car built by Kuhlman at the request of the Cleveland Underground Subway Company in 1913. The motorman had his own compartment and his own door for unloading at high-platforms. This one-of-a-kind unit had the Kuhlman trademark center doors, albeit too narrow, and the Cleveland Railway Scullin louver roof, but also had window guards to protect hands from subway walls and an air whistle for warnings in the subway. *(Cleveland Railway photo, Blaine Hays collection)*

Even some older streetcars were run in trains, as shown here entering the Luna Park loop in 1916. Cars are 759 and 343. *(Harry Christiansen photo, Blaine Hays collection)*

The Bus Operations of Cleveland Railways

Peter Witt was an intense man with very definite ideas. He had been quite emphatic in 1915, stating that the principle of transit service must be that it "shall be rendered at cost." This led Witt, after World War I, when no longer street railway commissioner, to experiment with the development of motor buses to see what role they might play in reducing transit costs. He observed, "Between the car riders who own the streets, and private companies having tracks therein, a constant, and at times a bitter, struggle takes place. The spring from which flows this stream of trouble is the failure of both to understand each other. The former demands a maximum service for a minimum fare, while the latter gives a minimum service for a maximum fare. Both are wrong!"

By the mid-1920's, Witt's experience resulted in a prototype 20-passenger lightweight motor bus which he produced privately. After working out several ideas for reducing vehicle weight and improving passenger capacity, he began producing his own design bus with his initials "PW" emblazoned across the motor's grill.

It is doubtful if any of these units were ever commercially sold, but they gave Witt an opportunity to make his point that public transit must be economically realistic to compete with other forms of transportation, namely the automobile!

The Cleveland Railway Company started a bus division in 1925 because of the threat of competition. In its selection of vehicles, it went completely opposite Peter Witt's thinking by purchasing longer and heavier buses.

The Kuhlman Car Company teamed up with fellow builder The White Company in the manufacture of buses. The sale of the Kuhlman car works to J. G. Brill of Philadelphia in 1904 and the death of G.C. Kuhlman in 1915 greatly changed the influence of the company in the industry. While still producing quality work, Kuhlman became known simply as "Brill of Ohio." In a practice of many years' duration, Kuhlman built bus bodies at the Collinwood shops, then shipped them by rail to the White factory at East 72nd Street and St. Clair Avenue where the bogies and chassis were fabricated and assembled. Similar arrangements were also made between White and the Lang Body Company of Cleveland.

The buses produced in this way not only gave Cleveland some distinctive types, but also made the city a leader in the city bus field. Cleveland Railway ordered its first big fleet of buses from White/Kuhlman in late 1925. These hood-in-front 29-seaters were numbered 100-159 and one of them, number 152, miraculously survived in Madison Township, near Cleveland, until the 1990's and then at RTA's Central Bus repair facility until finally scrapped in 1993.

In order to conserve space, the White Company developed a flattened motor which would take up less room under the body, enabling more capacity in less space. These motors became known as pancake engines and their application to Cleveland Railway buses 550-574 produced a 28' bus which was a perfect match to pull the locally fabricated Schult bus trailers during World War II.

To increase passenger capacity, John Stanley's thinking turned to the double deck bus, and Cleveland Railway bought a small fleet of double deckers in 1925. On the routes they plied, however, many special provisions had to be made, including trimming trees and lowering underpasses. Not only were the double deckers limited to a few routes with high clearances, the buses also required a two-man crew. The conductor operated a treadle-controlled rear door and the driver was responsible for a hand-operated front door. These drawbacks limited the use of the buses and reduced their desirability. One coach, number 509, was converted to a single-deck unit in 1931, but it proved cumbersome. The Great Depression was the fleet's undoing. After 1931 the double deckers only ran in rush hour, and all were out of service by January 1936.

The 20-passenger Peter Witt bus is displayed in front of the Art Museum about 1925. *(Peter Witt photo, Blaine Hays collection)*

This was Cleveland at its greatest glory--Public Square in 1925 with double and single deck buses, autos, classic architecture (Cuyahoga & Williamson buildings) and plenty of people boarding matching motor-trailer streetcars. This was the "metropolis" that inspired Jerry Siegel and Joe Shuster's *Superman* series. *(Cleveland Railway photo, Blaine Hays collection)*

White-Kuhlman bus 159 is seen at the Kuhlman plant when new in 1926. *(Blaine Hays collection)*

A White design of later years shows another distinctive style of the Cleveland builder. This 1947 model is departing Reed Garage for a trip on Scovill. *(Cleveland Transit photo, Blaine Hays collection)*

The double deck bus era is in full swing in Cleveland when this four-unit charter loads on East Sixth Street in 1929. An Indian motorcycle is parked in front of first bus. *(Cleveland Railway photo, Blaine Hays collection)*

Cleveland Transit Trade Shows

In 1920, Cleveland Railway celebrated its highest ridership to date — 327,840,438. It was also operating the new, fully-equipped Harvard Shops, one of the finest facilities of its kind in the world. Cleveland Railway was in the industry's limelight.

The Railway's accomplishments were highlighted by the Westinghouse Electric & Manufacturing Company, which in 1924 published a 67-page book, <u>The Cleveland Railway, The Story of its Operation and Maintenance.</u>

The result of this attention brought to Cleveland the 1926 American Electric Railway Association Convention. As company president and convention host, John Stanley made a triumphant entry in a horse-drawn wagon. Ten hours later Stanley collapsed and died during the evening session, which threw the entire convention into mourning. He had lived long enough, however, to see the fruits of his labor. It would later be said that John Stanley was one of the bright lights in the development and management of electric railways in the country.

The electric railway industry at this time was at its peak, and the featured equipment reflected this. On display were very few buses, but many city trolley cars and plenty heavyweight interurban equipment. The only indication of the coming change in vehicle design was the appearance of many lighter-weight city trolleys. These foreshadowed a complete transformation in the transit industry which would take place between the 1926 and 1934 A.E.R.A. conventions in Cleveland when buses, trackless trolleys, and Electric Railway Presidents' Conference Committee type streetcars would dominate the scene.

John Stanley had done such a thorough job of arrangements for the trade group that the 1926 show was called the "finest preparation ever made to receive the Association" and resulted in its returning to Cleveland in 1927 and 1928.

Prior to its return, however, Cleveland Railway was a major participant in the Cleveland Industrial Exposition of 1927, which spotlighted Cleveland's automobile industry. The transit company's advertising could not ignore the auto, stating "Both the automobile and the streetcar are essential to the progress and convenience of every metropolitan community." Not surprisingly, however, Cleveland Railway concluded, "Even if you own an automobile, take a streetcar."

The company's outdoor exhibit on East Third Street featured its new home-built motor-trailer streetcars, numbers 1373 and 1995. Both units were equipped with axles and roller bearings from Canton's Timken Company. Destination signs on the cars proudly declared "One of 1600 Cars for Cleveland Service."

Local suppliers were even more prominent upon the return of the A.E.R.A. delegates in 1927. Timken roller bearing trucks from Canton, Atlas Car and Manufacturing Company industrial hauling equipment from Cleveland, and Electric Railway Improvement Company (ERICO) electrical components from Solon all had impressive exhibits.

Lightweight cars received greater attention and included three classics: J.G. Brill's Master Unit, St. Louis Car's Rail Sedan, and Cincinnati Car Company's Curve Sider.

The 1928 show revealed the strain of the industry, not yet in agreement about the need for an improved model trolley. The 1928 display included Twin Coach buses from Kent, Ohio; a Lake Shore Electric steel interurban car built in 1918; and several electric freight locomotives. Seven lightweight city cars and three trackless trolleys rounded things out. Differential Steel Car Company of Findlay, Ohio, showed off one of its three-unit dump trains. Most prominent, however, were Cleveland Railway's new Peter Witt motor car, number 333 (later 4000), and its 101-foot-long, three-truck articulated city car, both from Kuhlman.

The year following, 1929, the convention met in Atlantic City, New Jersey, and from that gathering came the Electric Railway Presidents' Conference Committee (ERPCC), a consortium of street railway executives and manufacturers committed to developing an ultra-modern street-car.

In spring 1934 Pullman constructed a prototype car embodying the findings of over three years of ERPCC research. Three other experimental cars were also built: another by Pullman; one by Twin Coach of Kent, Ohio; and one by J.G. Brill of Philadelphia. These four cars were brought to Cleveland for the A.E.R.A. convention in September 1934 and comprised the exhibit for that year's transit convention. It was the only occasion when all four experimental cars were together in one place.

Cleveland Railway, though an ERPCC member, was unable to muster the money to purchase PCC cars when they became commercially available. So though the cars made their debut in Cleveland, it would be some time before Clevelanders would have any to ride.

"One of the 1600 CARS *for* CLEVELAND SERVICE" is proclaimed on the roll sign of home-built exhibit car 1373 at the 1927 Cleveland Industrial Exposition. In addition to Timken Axles and bearings, the car was also equipped with Nuttal helical gears. Notice the extra wide front doors— a later refinement of the Peter Witt design. *(Cleveland Railway photo, Blaine Hays collection)*

Overview of exhibits on October 11, 1926, at the A.E.R.A. convention are a wooden 1914 - built Dump Freight, 021, built by Universal Dump Car Company; a Differential Steel Car Company Dump Motor built in 1925; and a 1921-built large steel Northern Ohio Traction & Light Company interurban car. Farther down the line is a Cincinnati-built lightweight interurban car. (*Cleveland* Press *photo, Blaine Hays collection*)

The view is southwest from next to Public Hall at the 1928 A.E.R.A. convention. Differential Steel Car Company of Findlay, Ohio, has one of its three-car dump trains on display. In the background are the new Kuhlman Peter Witt car prototypes — car 333 and articulated number 5000. The split destination signs were changed to single signs before being placed in service. (*Cleveland Railway photo, Edwin E. Allen collection*)

After the Electric Railway Presidents' Conference Committee conducted its three-and-a- half-year research project, experimental car, number 5300, known as the ERPCC Model "B" car, is shown emerging from the big doors of the Harvard Shops of Cleveland Railway in September 1934. *(Cleveland Railway photo, Blaine Hays collection)*

Using the technology developed by the ERPCC, Chicago Surface Lines asked two of the largest builders, Pullman and Brill, to build for them one car each. This is the "Brill-Chicago Car," built in Philadelphia for Chicago, at the display site in Cleveland in September 1934. Cleveland's three-year-old stadium provides the backdrop. *(Cleveland Railway photo, Blaine Hays collection)*

The Articulated Streetcar Fleet

It was appropriate that Euclid Avenue, one-time Cleveland's Millionaires' Row, and then later its prime shopping street and busiest transit line, should receive the city's largest and most impressive streetcar. The fleet of 28 articulated cars, numbered 5000-5027, began serving the avenue in October 1927.

An articulated car is actually a double car with a narrow passage allowing passengers to move between the front and rear units. It was an improvement over the trailer car in which crowded passengers were unable to move from a more crowded unit to a less crowded one. Cleveland's articulateds were also better able to carry heavy loads since their middle truck was motorized, giving them three traction motors compared to the two on a motor-trailer train.

Cleveland's articulated fleet was built by the Kuhlman Car Company, and it was put into service between 1927 and 1929, operating out of Windermere Station. With electric heat and comfortable leather seats, the cars were quite popular with riders. Youngsters particularly enjoyed riding in the swiveling drum that connected the front and back units. The articulateds were also popular with transit management because they were real crowd swallowers. The lumbering giants were 101.2 feet in length and could seat 100 passengers. Including standees, they could handle about 250 passengers. By comparison, the 5000s were 24 feet longer than the modern articulated cars that currently run on the Regional Transit Authority's Shaker lines.

The 5000s were designed for the heavy traffic of Euclid Avenue, but after the Great Depression struck and ridership fell, most of the fleet were assigned to the Detroit Avenue line, running out of Rocky River Station, with just a few cars reserved for rush hours service on Euclid Avenue. With the upsurge of riding that came with World War II, the fleet was returned to Euclid in 1942 and served out the rest of its days in that service until the line was converted to diesel operation. The last car to operate was 5025, which was used in the Parade of Progress to commemorate the end of streetcar service on Euclid on April 27, 1952.

The Parade of Progress was a civic occasion sponsored by the Cleveland Transit System in partnership with many other Cleveland organizations. The participants provided floats or rolling exhibits for the parade, with the centerpiece being one each of all the types of extant streetcars and a line of new buses.

The parade meant the final run for many one-of-a-kind examples of street railway technology which had meant so much to the refinement of transit in Cleveland a half-century before. The life's work of people long committed to history, like John Stanley, Peter Witt, Gustave Kuhlman, J.A. Mehling, and Terrance Scullin were paraded one final time before the citizenry at the event before being offered to the scrap heap. A crowd of about 300,000 lined the avenue that Sunday to watch history passing before their eyes.

Cleveland Transit officials were hoping that the articulateds, with less than 25 years of service, might be sold to another transit operator. No bids for the fleet were forthcoming, however, and the cars were scrapped at the agency's Harvard Yard in 1953.

Passengers could walk between front and rear sections of Cleveland's articulated fleet, which were joined by a swiveling drum section. The conductor's station is at the left. *(Cleveland* Press *photo, Jim Toman collection)*

CTS articulated 5014 is passing the Allen Theater in Playhouse Square. The articulated cars often picked up crush loads at the East 14th Street stop as movie-goers left the theaters. *(Anthony Krisak photo, Richard Krisak collection)*

CTS 5018 is on its way downtown on Euclid Avenue at about East 120th Street. Lakeview Cemetery is is the background. *(Jim Spangler photo)*

Cleveland Railway articulated car 5019 sports its new Raymond Loewy green-gray-white paint scheme in Rocky River Station in 1940. The jumbo streetcars were then serving on the Detroit Avenue line. *(Jim Spangler collection)*

In the Parade of Progress, highfloor car 0649, renumbered from ten-hundred type car number 1000, still has its Scullin louver roof but also plenty of rust. *(Ross Barnard photo, Blaine Hays collection)*

The more modern buses in Parade of Progress order are: White 2950, Mack 2707, GMC 3629, and Twin Coach 3785, fueled by propane. The scene is at East Sixth Street. *(Ross Barnard photo, Blaine Hays collection)*

The PCC Car

The Presidents Conference Committee (PCC) streetcar was the street railway industry's attempt to design a modern rail vehicle that would be able to withstand the challenges presented by the automotive age. In Cleveland, riders gave the sleek and quiet cars high marks, but by the time the first PCC cars arrived for regular service in the city, the Cleveland Transit System (CTS) had already decided to end all streetcar operations.

The first PCC cars in the nation went into revenue service in Brooklyn, New York, in 1936. Except for a brief period in 1938 when the Cleveland Railway Company had tested a borrowed Pittsburgh Railways Company PCC, Clevelanders had to wait until 1946 before they had PCC cars of their own to ride.

In its 1944 plan to modernize the system, CTS had envisioned a PCC-based system entering the central business district via private right of way and operating there in a central subway. To fulfill this plan it placed its first order for 50 PCCs from Pullman-Standard in March 1945. By May 1946, however, the CTS board had decided on an alternate modernization plan that would end all surface streetcar operations in favor of a single crosstown high-platform rapid transit line.

So when the PCCs cars arrived in Cleveland, they were in fact an orphan fleet. The new cars went into revenue service on Superior and St. Clair avenues on October 1, 1946, and passengers found them a pleasant improvement over the older style cars. In response to complaints from west side riders and officials who resented the streamliners being assigned to the east side, CTS reluctantly secured another 25 St. Louis Car Company PCCs in a trade with Louisville, Kentucky, which had ordered the cars but then decided to abandon rail operations. That brought the CTS fleet to 75 streamliners, with some of them assigned to the West 25th Street car line.

By fall 1952 CTS found in the Toronto Transit Commission a willing buyer for its slightly used PCC fleet, and the cars ran there until 1982. The last PCC to operate over Cleveland streets was car 4223, a charter over the system's remaining trackage on March 8, 1953.

Clevelanders still had PCC cars, though. The Shaker Heights Rapid Transit bought 25 new cars from Pullman-Standard in 1948, and then later it purchased additional used PCCs from the Twin Cities and St. Louis for its fleet. SHRT even bought back nine of the old Cleveland PCCs from Toronto in 1978. PCCs ran on the Shaker lines until December 1984, when the last car was finally retired.

PCC 4210 is on a reserved center strip of Brookpark Road, heading for the West 33rd Street loop in Broadview Road service. September 1949. *(Jim Spangler photo)*

Four years after the 1934 American Transit Association convention in Cleveland, Cleveland Railway wanted to take a more serious look at the PCC car and was able to borrow Pittsburgh Railways car 1095, which was regauged and painted in the new Cleveland Railway green and gray scheme. It is on display in Public Square. *(Blaine Hays collection)*

PCC 4217 stops for passengers on East 55th Street just south of Broadway Avenue. The car is in short turn service to Chard Loop. *(Anthony Krisak photo, Richard Krisak collection)*

PCC 4206 is leaving Euclid Beach loop in special service. Streetcars served Euclid Beach Park via the St. Clair line until April 1951. *(Bruce Young collection)*

A St. Louis Car Company PCC, CTS 4257, is headed downtown on St. Clair Avenue at East 55th Street. Passenger islands were a common safety feature at busy stops.   *(Anthony Krisak photo, Richard Krisak collection)*

The Trackless Trolley

Transit patrons along Payne and Hough avenues must have given a second look to the clumsy vehicles that stopped for them on February 26, 1936. Boxlike in appearance and with two trolley poles mounted on the roof drawing power from a double-wire overhead system, the fleet of 20 Pullman-Standard trackless trolleys (called the "trackless electric car" by Cleveland Railway) that began operating in Cleveland that day had none of the grace that marked the system's most recent streetcars.

It was Clevelanders' first experience of the electric-powered, rubber-tired vehicle. The TTs were on the Hough line, and they were replacing buses, which had replaced streetcars on the Payne Avenue a year before to permit installation of new sewer lines. The city had to repave those streets and was awaiting a reply from the company on its share of track renewal costs. Instead the company made the decision to convert the service to trackless trolleys rather than invest in new tracks. Patrons must have liked the TTs, for ridership on the line increased significantly, and the following year eight more electric buses were added.

In 1940 Ohio builder Twin Coach Company of Kent decided to encourage the Cleveland Railway to develop more lines. It delivered its articulated Super-Twin trolley coach to Cleveland. Company executives liked the 47' 6" demonstrator which was being marketed as the "World's first Street Car on Pneumatic tires By Frank R. & William. B. Fageol." Cleveland Railway purchased the coach in 1942, and it became known to employees as the Queen Mary, the pride of the fleet.

The Hough trackless trolley line remained Cleveland's only one for nine years, but after World War II, as the Cleveland Transit System did away with its streetcars, 14 more TT lines were added. They then became a familiar sight to Clevelanders, and the coaches built by the Marmon Harrington Company even managed to look graceful.

Altogether there were four lines on the west side: Fulton, Clifton, Detroit, and Lorain. The east side had 11 lines: Hough, Wade Park, Cedar, Union, Broadway, East 105, Woodland, Buckeye, Kinsman, St. Clair, and Superior.

The trackless trolley era in Cleveland proved to be relatively brief. On November 14, 1958, the west side lines were converted to diesel bus operation. The conversion allowed CTS to utilize the substations that had carried power to the TT lines to be used to serve the rapid transit line's extension to West 143rd Street.

The east side lines lasted a little longer, but with ridership slipping, the Cleveland Transit System decided that it was no longer economically prudent to operate two different modes of surface transit. The first east side line to go was St. Clair in May 1962; it was followed by Buckeye, Woodland, and Kinsman in October. In April 1963 Superior, Wade Park, Hough, and Cedar went diesel. The last day for trackless trolleys in Cleveland came on June 14, 1963, when the Union, Broadway, and East 105th Street lines ran for the last time.

But that may not be the end of Cleveland's trackless trolley story. As part of its plan to improve operations on Euclid Avenue, the Regional Transit Authority has proposed replacing Euclid Avenue buses with trackless trolleys running in reserved lanes. If the federal government supports the plan, Cleveland will begin a second chapter in its trackless trolley history, and a new generation will experience the "bus with the poles on top."

Hough trackless trolley 923 is loading beside the federal court house on Public Square in the fall of 1939. It was the only trolleybus line in Cleveland until after the war. *(Cleveland Railway photo, Blaine Hays collection)*

In summer 1949 two Marmon-Harrington trackless trolleys are at East Ninth Street. TT 1274 (left) is coming out of Huron Road on the Broadway line. TT 1215 is on Prospect Avenue on the Woodland line. *(Jim Spangler photo)*

The poles are off the wire of CTS 6000, the system's only articulated trackless trolley. The August 1949 scene is at Hough Avenue and East 105th Street. *(Bill Vigrass photo)*

Clifton Boulevard trackless trolley 1028 is crossing West 25th Street on its way downtown in April 1958. It is about to cross the Detroit-Superior Bridge. *(Robert Runyon photo, Bruce Young collection)*

CTS 1221 in the system's new blue-and-white paint scheme is climbing Buckeye Road hill at Woodhill Avenue in January 1962. The crossing overhead wires serve the East 105th line. *(Herbert H. Harwood, Jr., photo)*

The Rapid Transit to Shaker Heights

To the modern ear, it would seem unlikely that plans for an upscale residential development would involve building a light rail line. Yet that was the factor that in 1920 brought the Greater Cleveland area its first rapid transit line.

In order to make travel between their new Shaker Heights community and downtown more convenient, Orris Paxton and Mantis James Van Sweringen knew that the existing surface streetcar lines would not do. As a result, they carved a private right-of-way for their Cleveland Interurban Railroad (CIRR) from Shaker Square (then called Moreland Circle) to downtown.

The CIRR started out in 1913 as a branch of Cleveland Railway's Fairmount line. It ran from Fairmount and Coventry to Shaker Boulevard and Fontenay Road. At about the same time the Vans also started construction on a more direct route from their model suburb to city center. It began operations on April 11, 1920. In Shaker Heights the line had two branches. One was built in the broad median strip of Moreland (now Van Aken Boulevard), the other in the Shaker Boulevard median. The two branches came together in Moreland Circle, and from there in private right-of-way made their way northwest, through Kingsbury Run to East 34th Street. There the line came to the surface and followed Cleveland Railway tracks to Public Square. Direct service to Cleveland Union Terminal began on July 20, 1930, when the Terminal Tower Complex was completed.

After the Van Sweringen empire collapsed during the Great Depression, the rapid transit line was operated on behalf of the bondholders, a consortium of Cleveland banks. Then in 1944, to save the line from being scrapped, the City of Shaker Heights purchased it, and it became known as the Shaker Heights Rapid Transit (SHRT). Municipal operation continued until September 5, 1975, when the rapid transit lines were absorbed into the new Greater Cleveland Regional Transit Authority.

In April 1980 RTA began a $100 million project to rebuild the deteriorating rail system, then renamed as the Blue (Van Aken) and Green (Shaker) lines. Partially closed down during the reconstruction period, the entire rebuilt system, with a new fleet of cars from Italy's Breda Costruzioni Ferroviarie, reopened for service on October 30, 1981.

Cleveland hosted the 1982 Rapid Transit Conference of the American Public Transit Association. At that event the rebuilding of the Shaker system was hailed as were the new Central Rail repair shops located near the main line at East 55th Street. The conference exhibit consisted of one of the new articulated low-platform rapid transit cars alongside RTA's 68-year-old historic streetcar, number 12, one of the 1914 Kuhlman center-entrance cars.

The Shaker rapid has been around long enough that it has seen transit fashions both come and go, and the line keeps rolling. Ridership remains steady, and RTA is currently studying the extension of the Blue Line to the Chagrin Highlands development.

Shaker Heights Rapid Transit car 18 glides through Shaker Square in January 1947. The center-entrance car, once the property of the Cleveland Railway Company, was one of a fleet of 32 which provided the bulk of Shaker service between 1920 and the advent of the PCC fleet. The last of this model was retired in 1960. *(Jim Spangler photo)*

Shaker PCC 88 travels through the mainline cut heading for the East 116th Street stop in March 1953. This car was part of a SHRT order of 25 PCCs from Pullman-Standard which went into service in 1948. (*Robert Runyon photo, Bruce Young collection*)

Former Cleveland Transit System car 4238 went to Toronto in 1952. It returned to Cleveland in 1978 to provide rush hour help on the Shaker lines. Here it pauses in front of Lynnfield station in January 1979. *(Jim Spangler photo)*

Shaker Boulevard car 820 in Green Line service passes car 839 as it nears Coventry station in May 1994. The passing track area is located just east of Van Aken Boulevard. *(Jim Toman photo)*

The Cleveland Transit System Rapid

It was a banner day, March 15, 1955, as Cleveland joined the short list of American cities with a speedy high-platform rapid transit line. The city's three daily newspapers covered the event with special sections, and radio stations broadcast from the line's stations. Clevelanders felt pride in another "big city" achievement.

The rapid transit line was the culminating event in Cleveland Transit System's (CTS) post World War II modernization plan. As the war neared its end, CTS had begun making plans to modernize the transit system. In 1946 the CTS board approved a plan based on the recommendations of the DeLeuw Cather consulting firm from Chicago. It called for surface operation by rubber-tire vehicles only and a single crosstown rail rapid transit line running from Windermere to West 117th Street. The plan also called for the rapid transit line to operate in a five-station downtown subway loop to be built somewhat later.

Partially financed by a $29.5 million loan from the federal Reconstruction Finance Corporation, CTS had to keep total costs in check, and so the rapid was built along existing railroad corridors, and it followed the basic configuration of a line laid out earlier by the Van Sweringen brothers. Construction began in February 1952.

The rapid transit opened in two stages. The March 1955 opening was for the segment between Windermere and Cleveland Union Terminal. The west side branch, between the Terminal and West 117th Street, did not open until August 14, 1955. Running time for the east side branch was 18 minutes, and for the west side 12 minutes. From end to end, 13.1 miles, running time represented about a half-hour savings in travel time over the surface routes.

Originally the rapid transit line had 12 stations and was served by a fleet of 68 cars (56 of them double units) built by the St. Louis Car Co. The rapid was subsequently extended to West 143rd Street in 1958 and then out to Cleveland Hopkins International Airport in 1968. These extensions, together with a new station at East 34th Street, brought the rapid to 19.1 miles and 18 stations.

The rapid transit fleet has been modernized twice. In 1967, to prepare for the airport opening, CTS purchased a fleet of 20 cars from Pullman-Standard and later added 10 more. Then in 1984 a new fleet of 60 cars from the Tokyu Car Company began to arrive, allowing the older units to be retired.

The downtown distributor subway, although approved by voters in 1953, was not built. It was vetoed by the Board of Cuyahoga County Commissioners at the urging of County Engineer Albert Porter, who had advocated that county resources should be used for highway improvements, not for public transit. That decision left the rapid transit line with only the single Union Terminal station and thus limited the line's appeal to riders who were working or shopping away from Public Square.

A four-car train of St. Louis Car Company-built rapid cars is at the East 55th station. The train is heading for West 117th Street. The rapid transit line on the east side used left-side running until a new station was built in Tower City in 1990. *(Ben Rohrbeck photo)*

In May 1990 Tokyu-built rapid transit car 304 is passing through Kingsbury Run, heading west. The next stop is East 55th Street. *(Jim Toman photo)*

In 1977 a Pullman-built RTA Airporter car stops at the East 34th Street-Campus station on its way to Windermere. The car is in left-hand running. *(Jim Toman photo)*

The Waterfront Line

To help celebrate the city's bicentennial in 1996, the rail rapid transit system grew a bit. The Waterfront line, as that extension of rail service is known, began operations on July 10, 1996.

Since 1968, when the rapid transit extension to Cleveland Hopkins International Airport opened, there had been no addition to Cleveland's rail network. Proposals for new lines had come and gone, but the system remained unchanged. One idea, however, had managed to plant a seed. It had called for a Flats trolley line, using vintage streetcars, which would serve the rapidly developing night life district. Out of that idea the Waterfront line grew. Construction on the new line began in September 1994.

The Waterfront Line is operated as an extension of the Regional Transit Authority's low-platform Blue and Green lines which operate between Shaker Heights and downtown Cleveland. Until 1996, the lines' downtown terminus had been the Tower City Center (formerly Cleveland Union Terminal) station. From Tower City the new line curved down into the Flats, and then crossed the lakefront railroad tracks before turning eastward to end in the municipal parking lot at about East 14th Street.

The 2.2-mile extension included four new stations: Settlers Landing and Flats East Bank in the Flats, North Coast (East Ninth Street), and South Harbor (the parking lot). In 1999 a fifth station was added to serve the new Cleveland Browns Stadium at West Third Street.

Built at a cost of $69.5 million, the Waterfront line opened with a flourish, carrying crush loads during the Bicentennial celebrations in the Flats. The line should also prove quite popular with Browns' fans, as parking for the new stadium is quite limited.

The ultimate utility of the line, however, probably depends on its being extended southward from its present parking lot terminus, and in 1999 Regional Transit Authority planners are studying ways in which an extension of the line could serve patrons of the Playhouse Square theaters and students on the Cleveland State University and metro Cuyahoga Community College campuses, before looping farther south and back onto the main tracks in the vicinity of East 22nd-East 30th Street.

If the Waterfront line gets its new trackage sometime during the first decade of the 21st century, it would restore "streetcars" (that is what modern light rail vehicles really are) once again to downtown Cleveland streets, and the streetcar's warning gong would be heard there once again after an absence of more than 50 years.

A two car train in RTA's special bicentennial paint approaches South Harbor Station on the Waterfront line in July 1996. RTA painted five cars for the opening which coincided with the city's bicentennial celebrations. *(Jim Toman photo)*

A Waterfront train is about to pass beneath the Memorial Shoreway as it heads for the East Ninth Street Station. In the background (right) is the Celebrezze Federal Office Building and North Point (left). *(Jim Toman photo)*

A Waterfront car is on the trestle above Front Avenue. The trestle carries the line over the lakefront railroad tracks. February 1998. *(Jim Toman photo)*

**OTHER CLEVELAND BOOKS AVAILABLE AT YOUR BOOKSTORE
OR BY MAIL FROM CLEVELAND LANDMARKS PRESS, INC.**

CLEVELAND STADIUM: THE LAST CHAPTER, a history of the old Cleveland Municipal Stadium from planning through demolition; soft cover, 135 pages, 140 illustrations, $24.50 (+$3.50 shipping)

WHEN CLEVELAND HAD A SUBWAY, a photo essay on the streetcar subway on the lower deck of Detroit-Superior (Veterans Memorial) Bridge; soft cover, 48 pages, 45 illustrations, $8.95 (+ $3.00 shipping)

FUMBLE! THE BROWNS, MODELL AND THE MOVE, an analysis of what went wrong for the Browns that led to their leaving in 1995; hard cover, 331 pages, 50 illustrations, $24.00 (+3.50 shipping)

CLEVELAND'S DYNAMIC TRANSIT HERITAGE, an illustrated review of Cleveland transit developments from horse car days through 1985; soft cover, 34 pages, 75 illustrations, $4.95 (+$3.00 shipping)

HORSE TRAILS TO REGIONAL RAILS, a complete history of public transit in Cleveland; hard cover, 376 pages, 332 illustrations, $49.00 (+ $4.00 shipping)

THE HEART OF CLEVELAND, the story of Public Square during the 20th century, the architectural developments on and around it, and the events that took place there; hard cover, 144 pages, 150 illustrations, $28.50 (+ $4.00 shipping)

CLEVELAND'S TRANSIT VEHICLES, an illustrated description and roster of Cleveland's public transit equipment; hard cover, 288 pages, 142 illustrations, $47.00 (+4.00 shipping)

CLEVELAND LANDMARKS PRESS, INC.
13610 Shaker Boulevard, Suite 503
Cleveland, Ohio 44120-1592